Monkey Tales

by Claire Daniel
illustrated by Baldo Aponte

Scott Foresman
is an imprint of

PEARSON

Glenview, Illinois • Boston, Massachusetts • Chandler, Arizona •
Upper Saddle River, New Jersey

Photographs

Every effort has been made to secure permission and provide appropriate credit for photographic material. The publisher deeply regrets any omission and pledges to correct errors called to its attention in subsequent editions.

Unless otherwise acknowledged, all photographs are the property of Pearson Education, Inc.

22 Jupiter Images.

ISBN 13: 978-0-328-52674-1
ISBN 10:   0-328-52674-6

Copyright © by Pearson Education, Inc., or its affiliates. All rights reserved. Printed in the United States of America. This publication is protected by copyright, and permission should be obtained from the publisher prior to any prohibited reproduction, storage in a retrieval system, or transmission in any form or by any means, electronic, mechanical, photocopying, recording, or likewise. For information regarding permissions, write to Pearson Curriculum Rights & Permissions, One Lake Street, Upper Saddle River, New Jersey 07458.

Pearson® is a trademark, in the U.S. and/or in other countries, of Pearson plc or its affiliates.
Scott Foresman® is a trademark, in the U.S. and/or in other countries, of Pearson Education, Inc., or its affiliates.

3 4 5 6 7   V0N4   17 16 15 14 13 12 11 10

One hot afternoon, Monkey, Snake, Hyena, Leopard, Elephant, Turtle, and Zebra took protection from the scorching noon sun under the lacy shade of an acacia tree.

"That sun is so very hot," Hyena complained. "The only one of us who's cool is Crocodile over there in the water."

Everyone turned and looked enviously at Crocodile, who lounged in the muddy watering hole with only his eyes and nostrils showing above the water.

Monkey didn't want to lose anyone's attention to Crocodile, so he concluded that the best way to divert everyone's focus back towards himself was to tell a tale.

Monkey perched on one of the highest limbs of the acacia tree and looked down at his captive audience.

"Well, you know," said Monkey, in the tone of a wise sage, "there is a reason crocodiles hide in the water."

"Why is that?" Snake asked. Snake avoided the water most of the time. He slithered closer to Monkey to listen to the tale.

How the Crocodile Got His Skin

"A long time ago, crocodiles had skin the color of wheat. One crocodile was very proud of his skin, and each evening he would lie next to the watering hole and show himself to all the animals in the forest.

"Sure enough, when all the monkeys, giraffes, hyenas, zebras, snakes, baboons, and even elephants came to the watering hole for their evening drink, they also admired the crocodile and his golden skin. Everyone complimented him, cooing how smooth and soft his skin was."

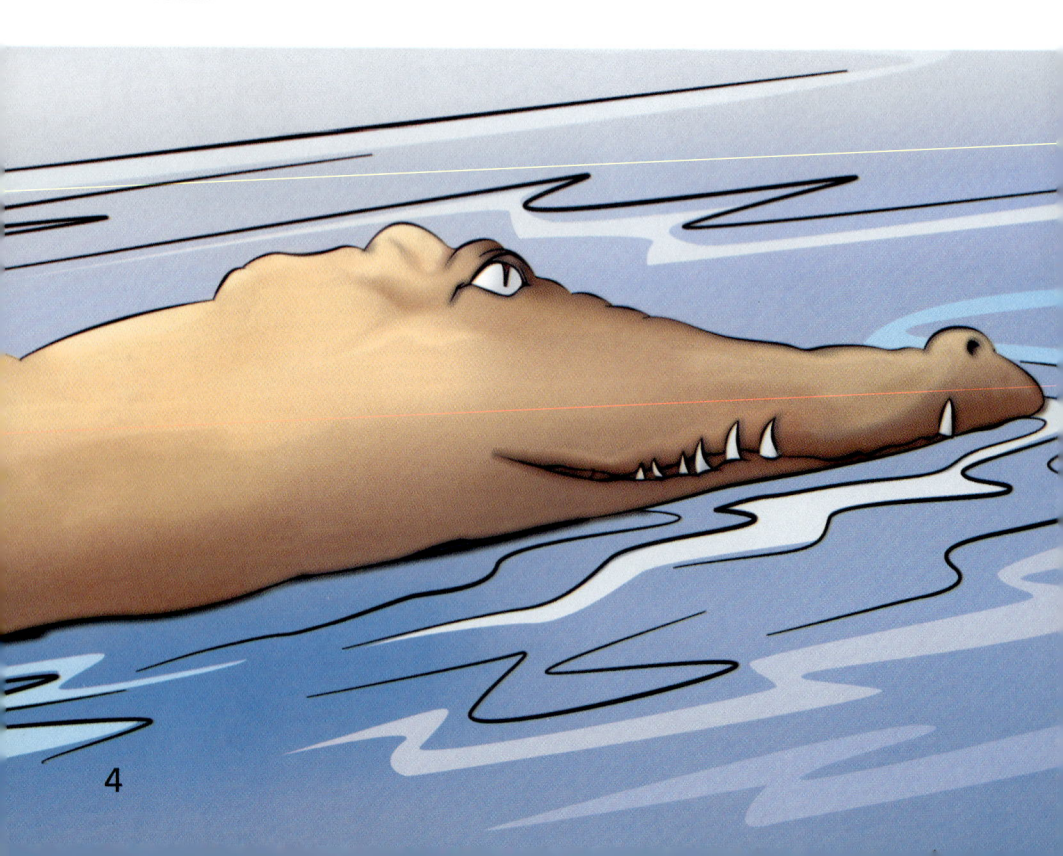

"But the crocodile wasn't satisfied with having the animals admire him only at night. So he began sunning himself during the day.

"All day long, and even on the hottest days, the crocodile would sit next to the watering hole so animals could come by and compliment him on his smooth, golden skin. He loved being admired. Periodically, some of the animals warned the crocodile that sunning himself might harm his skin, but the crocodile paid them no attention.

"As a result of his vanity, the crocodile's skin became rough, cracked, and ugly from all the exposure to the sun. The crocodile became so ashamed, that he disappeared into the water. To this day, he rarely comes out of the water to show himself."

All the animals laughed at Monkey's tale. Most of the animals were amazed at his wonderful explanation for something they had always wondered about.

5

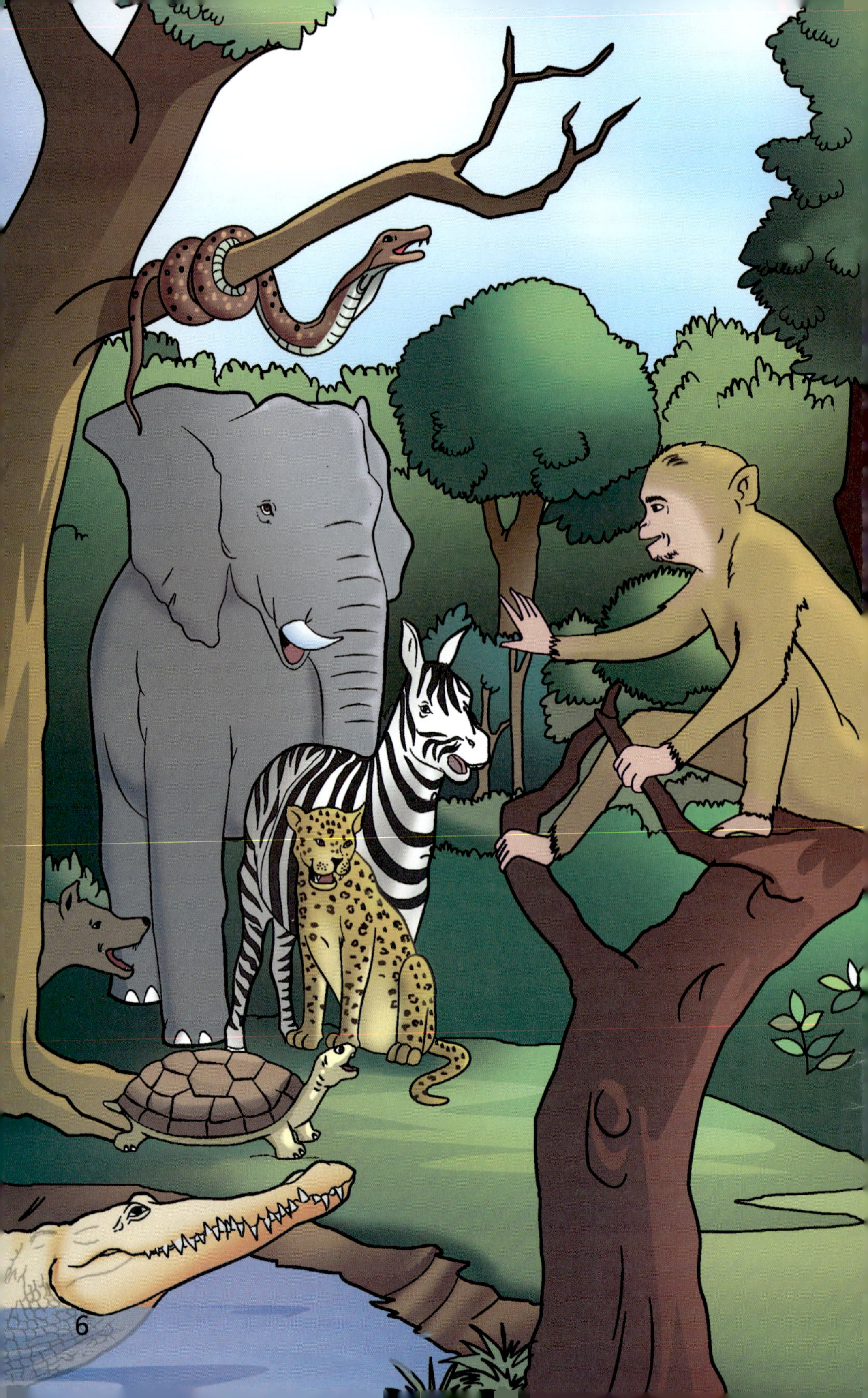

However, Crocodile did not look happy. He had never thought his skin was ugly before, and now he felt embarrassed.

"*I know a tale,*" Turtle offered eagerly.

But Monkey was not so willing to give up the attention. So he interrupted, "And I am just the one to tell it!" Monkey looked down at his audience and began again.

Why Turtles Live in Water

"Not so long ago, turtles used to live only on the land. One day, as several turtles were taking a leisurely stroll, one of the cleverer ones was trapped by some not-so-smart hunters." All the animals laughed in glee at the creature's carelessness and stupidity in being caught by the universally disliked hunters.

Monkey continued. "The hunters had already set a huge pot of water over the fire when they realized that none of them knew how to prepare the turtle for the soup. One hunter suggested cracking him open, but the clever turtle pointed out that he had a very hard shell."

"Finally the turtle advised, 'Why don't you just drown me? Throw me into the river, and then I'll be ready to be cooked in the pot.' So the hunters agreed and hurled the turtle into the river. The turtle, of course, could swim, and he swam as fast as he could to escape the hunters. From that day on, turtles have rarely ventured onto land."

All the animals cheered except for Turtle who sat quietly off to the side, feeling embarrassed.

Snake spoke up, for he had a great tale to tell that had been passed down from generations of snakes before him.

"I have a tale to tell," Snake said.

"Aha!" Monkey interjected. "I know that tale—and I'll save you the trouble of telling it."

"How could you, a *monkey*, know the *snake* tale I'm about to tell?"

"Because I do. And I bet that I, a *monkey*, will tell it better than you ever could!" Monkey boasted.

Poor Snake doubted very much that Monkey knew his tale or could tell it better than he could, but the other animals' cheering squashed his enthusiasm, and he gave into their pressuring. So Monkey began again.

Why Snakes Crawl

"Long ago, the rain stopped falling from the sky for many years. It had been so long since clouds had spilled raindrops that some children didn't even know what rain was. So one day Moon, who cared for all the animals, gathered them together. She told them that they must leave the land for it was becoming too dry and dangerous. She advised them to find another place to live where rain fell and grass grew.

"Everyone quickly packed all their belongings and prepared for their departure. The wildebeest packed up, the zebras made ready, and the ostriches gathered up their bags. Amidst all the confusion, Moon noticed that the snakes had not moved. Back in those days, snakes could walk, but that day the snakes were just sleeping lazily in the sand, wriggling their toes in the warmth of the sun. Moon asked them why they were not packing.

"The snakes responded, 'The rain will come back eventually—we don't know why you are fussing so. All of you go ahead, and we'll just wait here and save ourselves a lot of bother.'"

"It was well known that snakes were lazy creatures, so the animals left them and went to wetter and more fertile lands.

"At first, the snakes didn't mind being alone, but after a few weeks, they noticed that since all the frogs and mice had left, they had no food to eat.

"Without any moisture in the air, the snakes' scales became dry and irritated, and the sun began to bother them rather than soothe them as it once had. The snakes' stomachs made horrid noises, complaining loudly about their emptiness. Snake children cried all through the night for relief from their hunger pains. The snakes began to regret their decision."

"A week later, Moon reappeared, but by then the snakes had nearly perished. 'Help us!' the snakes beseeched Moon. Moon took pity on the snakes and agreed to help. The snakes looked down at their bodies and watched as their feet and legs disappeared. Their bodies lengthened, and their tails stretched much longer than they had been before.

"The snakes tried to move and found they could easily slide over the wide expanse of sand. While they were grateful that this new body used less energy to move and hunt, they looked down at their disfigured forms with disgust. From their once normal anatomy, they had transformed into slinky, slithering creatures.

"After the metamorphosis, they slithered along as Moon guided them along the path of the footsteps made by all the other animals until they reached safety and water. But snakes never, ever walked again."

Again, all the animals laughed and cheered—that is, all except Crocodile, Turtle, and Snake, who had all been embarrassed by Monkey.

Hyena was the next to speak up, and she whined in a loud voice, "I have a tale that is much better than all of those!"

"And who better than me to tell it?" Monkey cut in, laughing. Zebra and Leopard encouraged Monkey to go on and tell the next tale. Hyena sat quietly, her head down. She did not want to cross Monkey. Crocodile, Turtle, and Snake all groaned.

"Here we go again," Turtle grumbled, annoyed.

The Cloud Eaters

"Long ago, the jackal and the hyena both enjoyed eating clouds. They thought clouds were tastier than any food found on Earth, and to top it off, the view from the clouds was amazing. *From the clouds,* they said, *Sun and Moon are so nearby that we can almost reach the eaves of their house.*"

"However, cloud-eating was a tricky business. They could easily jump up into the clouds and stay while they were eating, but coming down was a different tale. The jump down was very far, and it was easy to slip off the cloud and plummet to the ground. So one day, rather than risking the long fall, the jackal asked the hyena to catch him after he ate his fill, and the hyena agreed.

"The jackal ate until his belly was filled with clouds, and finally he yelled down to the hyena that he was coming down. The hyena stretched out her arms and caught her friend safely.

"'It's my turn now,' the hyena said, and she jumped high into the air and landed on the densest cloud in the sky. She ate until she could eat no more and then yelled down to the jackal that she was ready to come down. The jackal nodded. But as he positioned himself to catch her, he stepped on a cactus and pierced his foot with a long, thick thorn. The jackal hopped away howling with pain."

"Hyena didn't know anything had occurred below her, and she took a big leap off the cloud! Without jackal to catch her, the hyena landed on the ground with a huge *THUD!!* And from that day on, hyenas' back legs have been shorter than their front legs," Monkey concluded.

Zebra and Leopard laughed as they stared at Hyena while Monkey finished up his tale. For the first time, all the animals, including Hyena, noticed that her back legs were indeed shorter than her front legs. Hyena hadn't even known this until that day, and she shrank from her friends in shame.

Leopard got excited. "I have a fabulous tale about a wise and courageous leopard."

Monkey interrupted, and said with a snicker, "I know this one, Leopard. It is indeed a good tale, but I wouldn't say the leopard in it was wise *or* courageous."

Leopard looked confused. "But . . ." And before Leopard could say anything further, Monkey was storytelling once again.

Leopard's Spots

"A long time ago, leopards were the same yellow-brown color as the desert. They had no spots, and they were considered to have the plainest fur coat of all the animals. One leopard in particular used to whine and complain about his fur to his friend the chameleon all the time. 'I wish I were more attractive like you,' he whimpered repeatedly.

"Even though the chameleon enjoyed hearing how beautiful she was, she was exhausted from her friend's bellyaching. So one day, as the leopard was complaining in his usual way, the chameleon offered him a solution.

"'Why don't you add some color to your coat?' he suggested. The leopard liked this idea.

"The next morning, the leopard went down to the bank of the watering hole and rubbed mud all over himself. Unfortunately, he couldn't reach his entire back, and since he didn't have any help, he missed patches here and there. But Leopard was too excited to notice, and he took off to find Chameleon to show her how beautiful he had become. But when she saw him, she gasped."

"'You have black spots,' she said haltingly. 'When I suggested adding some color to your coat, I was thinking about something a little bolder.' Only then did Leopard look down at his handiwork and see his mistake.

"'What have I done?' he wailed. But from that time forward, leopards have always had black spots."

Zebra rolled on the ground shaking with laughter, but Leopard looked horrified and embarrassed. That wasn't the tale he had planned to tell. That wasn't a good tale at all.

Zebra had a tale to tell, and she began to speak, but Monkey stopped her. "I know, I know," Monkey said laughing. "You, too, have a wonderful tale to tell. But do not tire yourself in the hot sun. I will tell your tale."

How Zebra got his Stripes

Monkey began, "It was another long, dry summer, and the water continued to evaporate until finally there was only one watering hole left for all the animals. Unfortunately, it belonged to an ancient baboon, the meanest animal around. Well Baboon decided to guard his watering hole so that it would be his and his alone. He built a fire beside the watering hole so he could see anyone coming, day or night.

"One late evening, a zebra approached the water and lowered her head down to drink. In those days, zebras' coats were the color of the clouds above, and zebras were very proud of being completely white. It was well known to everyone that the zebra would not only drink to her fill, but she would also take a bath to wash her pure white coat.

"'Stop!' the baboon shouted at the zebra, but she paid him no mind and dunked her head into the cool water. To defend what he felt was his, the baboon rushed at the zebra, and they were soon butting heads."

"Finally, the zebra turned her back on the baboon and kicked him clear of the watering hole. However, as she did so, she lost her balance and fell into the fire that was lit to guard the hole. Some of the charred sticks scraped the side of her body, and her beautiful white coat was now striped with black and white. Zebra coats have been that way ever since!" Monkey finished, triumphantly.

Everyone was silent. There wasn't even a hint of laughter. By then, Monkey had told tales about everyone except Elephant, and Elephant knew what he had to do.

"I have a tale," Elephant stated loudly, "but no one can tell it but me."

"I'm sure I know the tale, and I'm sure everyone would rather hear *me* tell it." Monkey beamed with pride.

"NO!" Elephant boomed and then continued calmly, "I'll be telling this one."

"Oh, boy," Monkey sneered, irritated that he was no longer the center of attention, but also a little nervous after Elephant's forceful rejection. "I am sure no one wants to hear your tale."

"Oh, no, we do!" all the animals insisted. They were tired of Monkey's less-than-complimentary tales.

"Very well," Elephant said. "I think everyone will enjoy this tale."

Why Monkeys Live in Trees

"In the old days, when crocodiles had golden skin, turtles lived on land, snakes could walk, hyenas' legs were all the same length, leopards had plain fur, and zebras were entirely white, monkeys lived in caves. At the time, monkeys had a close relationship with the elephants.

"One day, an elephant and a monkey went to the market to buy a cow. They saw the fattest cow they had ever seen, and they both wanted it. The elephant offered to share the cow with the monkey, but the monkey wouldn't hear of it. The monkey wanted the cow for himself. So the monkey secretly promised the cow seller one of the elephant's ivory tusks if he could have the entire cow. The cow seller agreed.

"The next morning the elephant woke up to find her tusk missing. She was very upset and went to talk with her friend, the monkey. When she arrived at the monkey's house, he wasn't there. The elephant sat down and waited for her friend. Hours later, the monkey, whistling happily, returned with the cow. The monkey was shocked to see his friend sitting in his home."

"Once the elephant saw the cow, she knew exactly what had happened to her tusk. She was so angry she chased the monkey for miles until the monkey finally escaped into the trees. Monkeys have lived in trees ever since."

All the animals cheered. "That was the best tale we heard all day," laughed Zebra.

"I agree," replied Turtle.

"Me too," chimed Hyena.

"The best," added Leopard.

Snake turned to Monkey and asked, "Wasn't that a great tale?"

Monkey's face turned white, and then red, and then green. He was so angry that someone had told an embarrassing tale about him that he stomped away. But to this day, he has never told an embarrassing tale about another animal again.

21

Pourquoi Stories

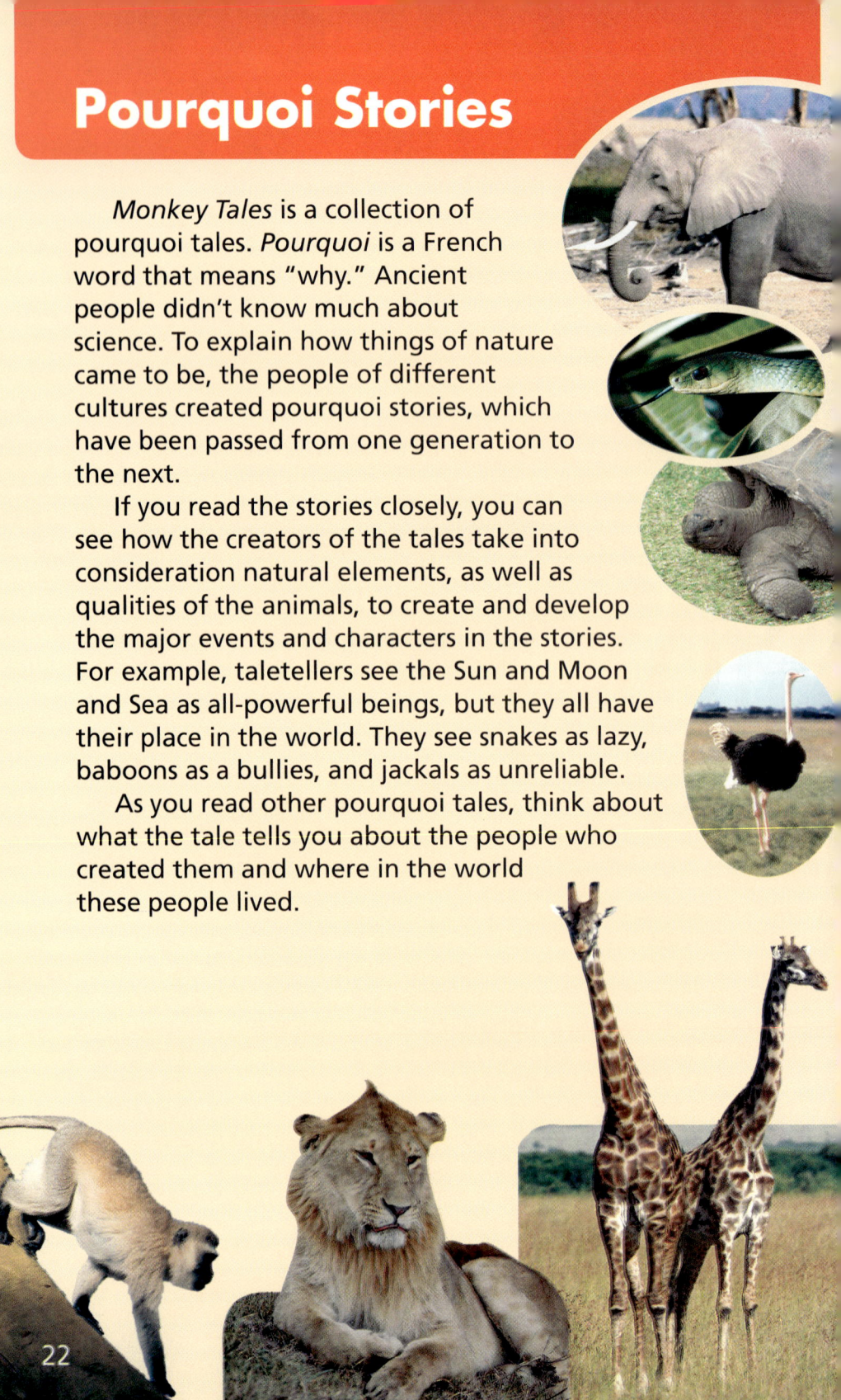

Monkey Tales is a collection of pourquoi tales. *Pourquoi* is a French word that means "why." Ancient people didn't know much about science. To explain how things of nature came to be, the people of different cultures created pourquoi stories, which have been passed from one generation to the next.

If you read the stories closely, you can see how the creators of the tales take into consideration natural elements, as well as qualities of the animals, to create and develop the major events and characters in the stories. For example, taletellers see the Sun and Moon and Sea as all-powerful beings, but they all have their place in the world. They see snakes as lazy, baboons as a bullies, and jackals as unreliable.

As you read other pourquoi tales, think about what the tale tells you about the people who created them and where in the world these people lived.